SEE-THROUGH
SHARKS

STEPHEN SAVAGE
ILLUSTRATED BY ROD FERRING

RUNNING PRESS
KIDS

9   8   7   6   5   4   3   2   1
Digit on the right indicates the number
of this printing

Library of Congress
Control Number: 2005922012

ISBN 0-7624-2720-5

This book was created by
THE IVY PRESS LIMITED
The Old Candlemakers
West Street, Lewes BN7 2NZ

PUBLISHER   Alastair Campbell
EXECUTIVE PUBLISHER   Sophie Collins
CREATIVE DIRECTOR   Peter Bridgewater
EDITORIAL DIRECTOR   Jason Hook
DESIGN MANAGER   Simon Goggin
SENIOR PROJECT EDITOR   Caroline Earle
DESIGNER   Wayne Blades
ILLUSTRATOR   Rod Ferring

This book may be ordered by mail from the
publisher. Please include $2.50 for postage and
handling. But try your bookstore first!

Running Press Book Publishers
125 South Twenty-second Street
Philadelphia, Pennsylvania 19103-4399

Visit us on the web!
www.runningpress.com

CONTENTS

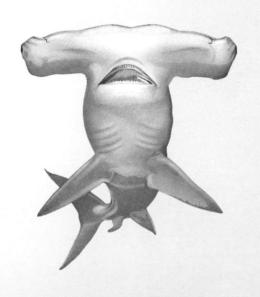

WHAT IS A SHARK?

For many people the word "shark" conjures up the stuff that nightmares are made of—the huge jaws of the great white shark opening to display terrifying rows of razor-sharp teeth. A shark's fearsome appearance is inherited from ancestors that lived in the oceans millions of years ago. When these sharks roamed the oceans, dinosaurs still roamed the land. Although millions of years have now passed, many sharks have changed little in all that time. Today, they are one of the most successful oceanic predators. Like fish, sharks are vertebrates (have a backbone), breathe using gills, and have fins to help them move. But while not all sharks conform to our nightmare image of them, they all have unique features that only sharks and their close relatives share.

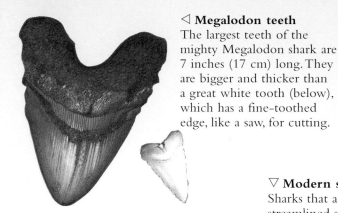

◁ **Megalodon teeth**
The largest teeth of the mighty Megalodon shark are 7 inches (17 cm) long. They are bigger and thicker than a great white tooth (below), which has a fine-toothed edge, like a saw, for cutting.

FLEXIBLE SKELETONS
Unlike other fish, which have skeletons made of bone, sharks have skeletons made of cartilage. This is a tough, flexible substance that is lighter than bone. Rays also have skeletons made of cartilage. Together with sharks they are called cartilaginous fish.

CLUES TO THE PAST
Scientists have found out about prehistoric sharks from fossils of their teeth that have turned to stone. Teeth are the most common shark fossils. The 40-foot (12-meter) long Megalodon shark lived 10–25 million years ago. Almost all we know about this shark, which is similar to a great white, comes from teeth and a few vertebrae.

▽ **Modern shape**
Sharks that are this typical streamlined shaped are, in evolutionary terms, the newest species.

MODERN SHARKS
Larger, predatory sharks probably started to grow in numbers about 60 million years ago, when whales and other sea mammals appeared in the oceans. Fossilized teeth from large sharks are often found alongside the bones of sea mammals that have been chewed by the sharks.

THE FIRST SHARK?
One of the earliest sharks was Cladoselache, which lived before the age of the dinosaurs. The Hybodant shark became extinct about the same time as the last dinosaurs. These early sharks were replaced by larger predatory sharks—sharks that prey on other animals for their food.

△ **Cladoselache**
This 3.3-foot (1-meter) long prehistoric shark lived in the oceans 400 million years ago. It has the features of an active hunter.

▷ **Shark fossils**
Whole body fossils, like this Hybodant shark fossil, are rare because when a shark dies, its cartilaginous skeleton quickly disintegrates.

SHARK SPECIES

There are over 350 different kinds or species of sharks found in all the world's oceans. Scientists divide them into eight main groups, called orders, depending on the features of their bodies. These include the body shape, the position of the fins, the shape of the tail, and whether there are backbones. Each order is made up of smaller groups, called families. Each family contains a number of species. Some families are bigger than others. For example, the dogfish family contains 72 species while the saw shark family only has five species. Shark experts do not know the exact number of species that exist and new ones are still being discovered.

Barbels

▽ **Shortnose saw shark**
Saw sharks often rest on the seabed. They use the two long barbels on their snout to root out small fish hiding in the sand.

SHARP SNOUTS
The saw sharks are a family of sharks with long, bladelike snouts edged with teeth, which are used to slash at their fish prey. There are only five species in the saw shark family, which is the only family in the order pristiophoriformes.

LONG SNOUTS
Dogfish sharks, bramble sharks, and rough sharks are three families of sharks in the order squaliformes. Together they contain about 82 shark species that are found in all the world's oceans. They all have short mouths and long snouts.

△ **Prickly dogfish**
The bizarre-looking prickly dogfish is named after its prickly skin. It lives between 164 and 1,640 feet (50 and 500 meters) beneath the ocean's surface.

▽ **Bull shark**
Although no modern shark lives in fresh water, the bull shark can survive in rivers for several weeks.

BIGGEST GROUP
The largest and most dangerous group of sharks is called carcharhiniformes. It includes species from the small cat sharks to streamlined predators such as the tiger shark and the hammerhead. This order includes eight families with a total of 197 species.

△ **Angel shark**
Half buried in the sand on the seabed, an angel shark lies hidden from predators as it waits to lunge at passing fish.

FLATTENED BODIES
Angel sharks all have flattened bodies and large fins, which makes them look like rays. There are 12 species of angel sharks, in an order called squatiniformes. Their sandy-colored bodies help them hide on the seabed.

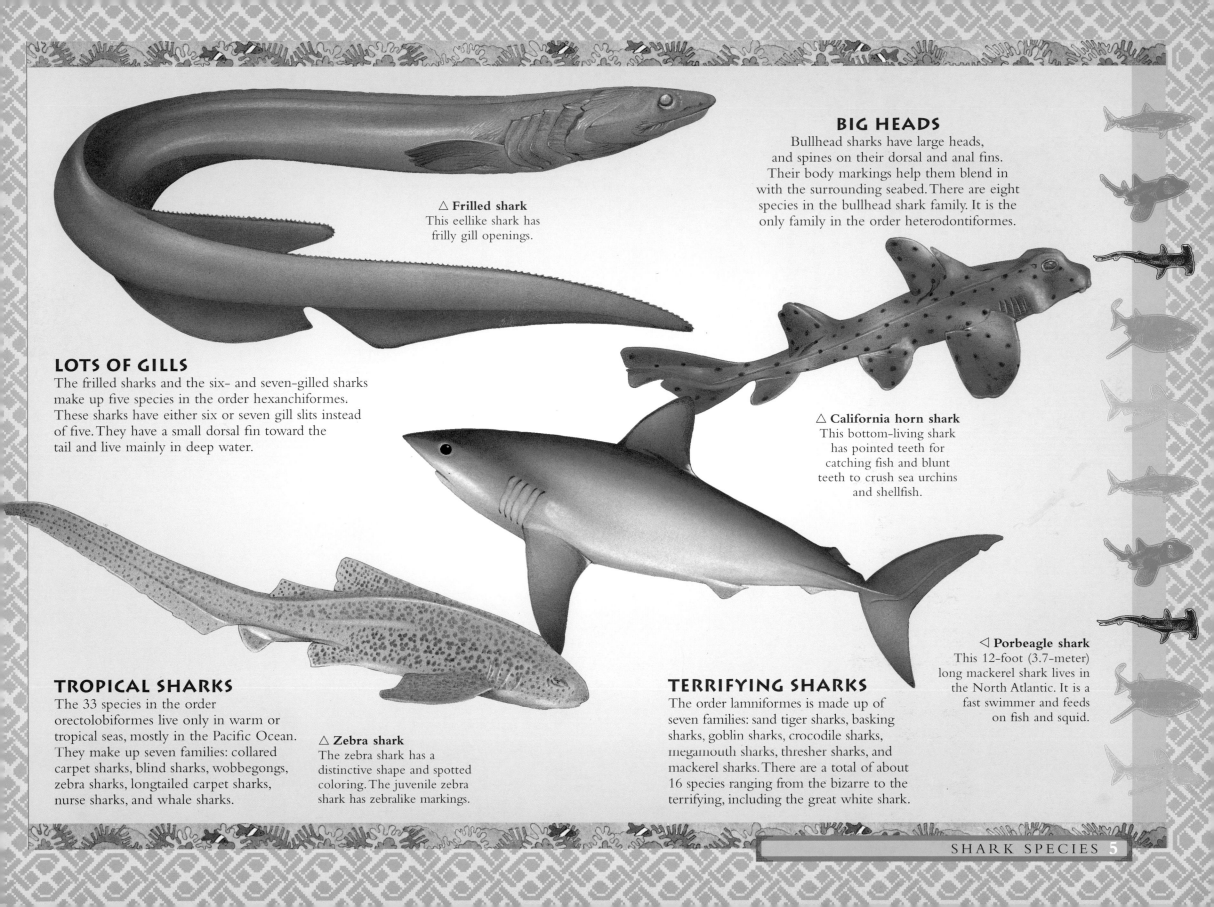

BIG HEADS

Bullhead sharks have large heads, and spines on their dorsal and anal fins. Their body markings help them blend in with the surrounding seabed. There are eight species in the bullhead shark family. It is the only family in the order heterodontiformes.

△ **Frilled shark**
This eellike shark has frilly gill openings.

LOTS OF GILLS

The frilled sharks and the six- and seven-gilled sharks make up five species in the order hexanchiformes. These sharks have either six or seven gill slits instead of five. They have a small dorsal fin toward the tail and live mainly in deep water.

△ **California horn shark**
This bottom-living shark has pointed teeth for catching fish and blunt teeth to crush sea urchins and shellfish.

◁ **Porbeagle shark**
This 12-foot (3.7-meter) long mackerel shark lives in the North Atlantic. It is a fast swimmer and feeds on fish and squid.

TROPICAL SHARKS

The 33 species in the order orectolobiformes live only in warm or tropical seas, mostly in the Pacific Ocean. They make up seven families: collared carpet sharks, blind sharks, wobbegongs, zebra sharks, longtailed carpet sharks, nurse sharks, and whale sharks.

△ **Zebra shark**
The zebra shark has a distinctive shape and spotted coloring. The juvenile zebra shark has zebralike markings.

TERRIFYING SHARKS

The order lamniformes is made up of seven families: sand tiger sharks, basking sharks, goblin sharks, crocodile sharks, megamouth sharks, thresher sharks, and mackerel sharks. There are a total of about 16 species ranging from the bizarre to the terrifying, including the great white shark.

GREAT AND SMALL

The oceans cover two-thirds of the Earth's surface and sharks can be found in them all. Sharks have bodies that are specially designed to survive in different temperatures and depths. Their shape and size is often linked to the type of prey they hunt. Many live in the open sea and have bodies that are designed for slow cruising or bursts of speed. Sharks that live on or near the seabed have flattened bodies that are specially colored to disguise them in the sand. A few shark species even live in the cold polar seas. Sharks that live in the deep oceans have some of the most bizarre body shapes of all.

▽ **Spiny pygmy shark**
A few species are incredibly small. The average length of the spiny pygmy shark is only 8 inches (20 cm).

SMALL SHARKS

About half of all living sharks are smaller than 3.3 feet (1 meter) in length. The average size for a shark, when fully grown, is 5 feet (1.5 meters). This may sound small until you consider that an average size person is 5 feet 8 inches (1.75 meters) tall. Most dangerous species are over 6.56 feet (2 meters) in length.

ODDITIES

Some of the strangest sharks live in the ocean depths. Their unusual body forms and bizarre-shaped heads resemble those of prehistoric sharks. Many deepwater sharks have only been discovered in recent years. The 16-foot (5-meter) long megamouth shark was first seen in 1976 and the goblin shark has rarely been seen alive.

△ **Goblin shark**
The paddle-shaped snout of the 10.8-foot (3.3-meter) long goblin shark helps it to find food.

HARMLESS GIANTS

Whale sharks (*see left*), basking sharks, and megamouth sharks are the harmless giants of the shark world. They engulf plankton and small fish with their huge, cavernous mouths. Whale sharks live in tropical seas, while basking sharks live in temperate seas.

△ **Whale shark**
At over 40 feet (12 meters) long, the whale shark is not only the biggest shark but also the largest fish.

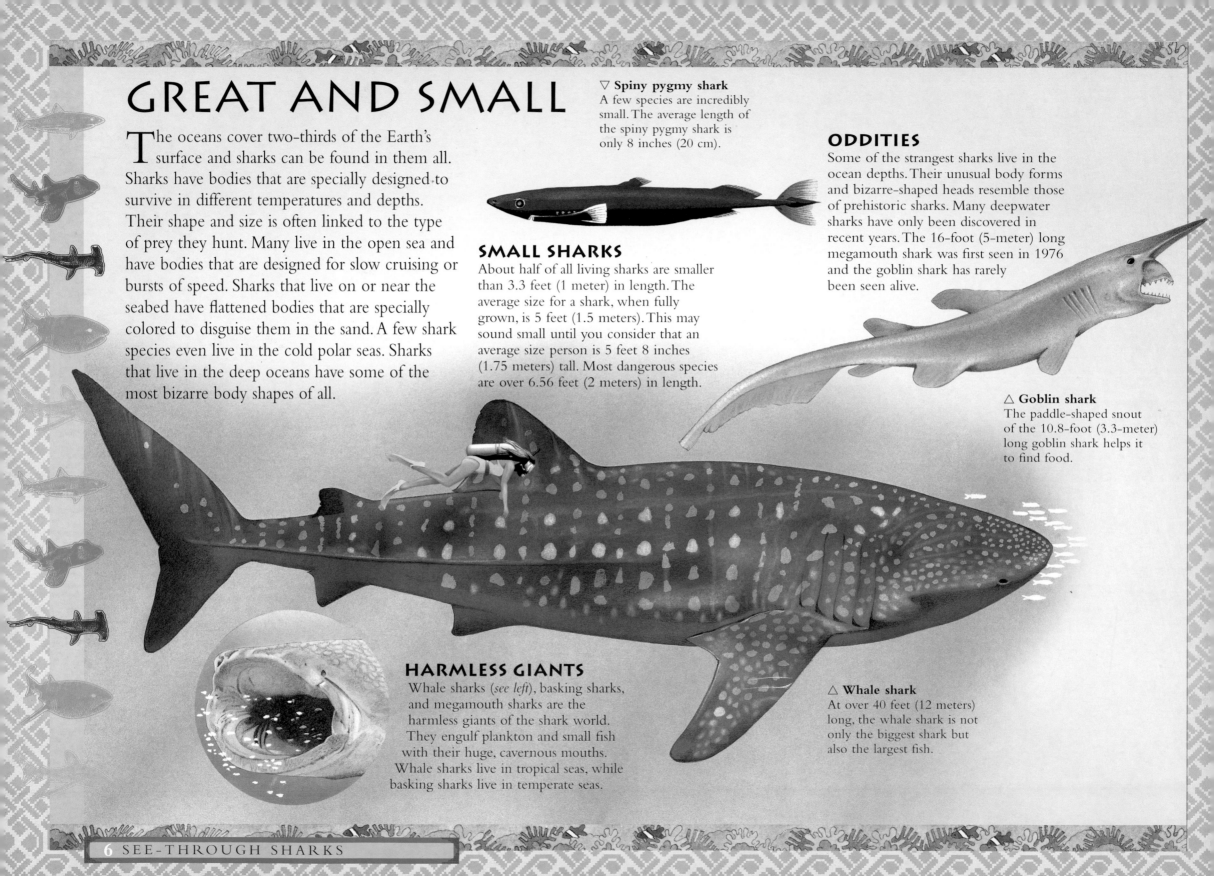

HAMMERHEAD

The head of the hammerhead shark has puzzled scientists for a long time. The hammer shape may give the shark more lift at the front of its body. It may also increase the shark's sensitivity to the Earth's magnetic field, which helps it to navigate (*see page 19*).

◁ **Scalloped hammerhead**
The scalloped hammerhead is one of nine species of hammerhead shark. It varies in length from 5 feet (1.5 meters) to 16 feet (5 meters).

SPEEDY SHARKS

Many sharks that live in the open sea have bodies that are designed for speed. Their bodies are a streamlined, torpedo shape, with a tapering head and snout. The forward thrust comes from the tail fins while the short stiff pectoral fins help the shark to maneuver at high speeds.

△ **Mako shark**
The mako is the fastest swimmer, reaching bursts of up to 22 miles an hour (35 km/hr). It can also leap 20 feet (6 meters) in an effort to escape when hooked on an angler's line.

LONG TAILS

Thresher sharks have the longest tails of all the sharks. The tail makes up half of the overall body length. The unequal shape of the tail is unusual for a fast swimmer, yet the thresher can swim fast and leap clear of the water.

▷ **Thresher shark**
The thresher shark uses its tail to herd together and stun its fish prey before eating it.

SHARK SAVVY

Depth Levels

Sharks live in different parts of the oceans, from shallow coastal waters to the dark ocean depths.

BLACKTIP SHARK	BLUE SHARK
OCEANIC WHITETIP SHARK	NURSE SHARK

330 FEET (100 METERS)

MEGAMOUTH SHARK

1,400 FEET (427 METERS)

LANTERN SHARK

3,300 FEET (1,000 METERS)

PYGMY SHARK

SHARK RELATIVES

Sharks are not the only fish that have a skeleton made of cartilage. Rays are another group of cartilaginous fish, which are closely related to sharks. There are almost 500 species of rays, which are thought to have evolved from flattened, bottom-dwelling shark species more than 150 million years ago. While they are related to sharks, rays have important features that make them different. Their bodies are highly flattened and their tail is long and thin. The pectoral fins have become much bigger to form a disk around the head. Chimera are also related to sharks. There are 35 different species of chimera, which are thought to have evolved from sharks about 340 million years ago.

CHIMERA
These bizarre-looking fish resemble their extinct ancestors, but appear quite different to both sharks and rays. Chimera have relatively large heads and bodies that are scaleless. A poisonous spine on the front of the dorsal fin can be used in self-defense.

△ **Longnose chimera**
This chimera is also known as a spookfish. The long snout has sensory pores to help it find prey.

△ **Plownose chimera**
This chimera has a specially designed snout to find invertebrates on the seabed.

▽ **Blue spotted stingray**
The colorful, 23-foot (7-meter) long blue spotted stingray lives on coral reefs in parts of the Pacific Ocean.

Pectoral fin

CHIMERA FEATURES
While most fish breathe by taking water to their gills through their mouth, chimeras have large nostrils that take water to the gills for breathing. Chimeras are slow swimmers. Species with elongated tails swim using pectoral fins at the front.

STINGS AND POISONS
Some rays have surprising methods of self-defense. Electric rays can stun prey and deter predators by giving them an electric shock. Stingrays have one or two poisonous spines on their tail that can be whipped around at an attacker.

RAYS
Most species of rays are adapted to live and feed near the seabed. Their mouth and gill slits are on the underside of the body. They breathe through spiracles behind the eyes, which are on the top of the head. This allows them to breath even when buried in the sand.

GIANT RAY

Not all species of ray live near the seabed. Some live in the open ocean. These include the biggest of all the rays, the harmless manta ray, which reaches over 21 feet (6.5 meters) wide. The large, fleshy extensions to the manta ray's wings are used to funnel plankton into its mouth.

△ **Manta ray**
The graceful manta ray swims with powerful strokes of its huge, winglike pectoral fins.

SAWFISH

Sawfish are a family of rays that are easily confused with saw sharks, because they both have saw-shaped snouts. One way to tell them apart is to look at the position of the gills, which are on the underside of the sawfish's body. Sawfish can be found in both fresh and saltwater.

◁ **Toothy weapon**
A sawfish can slash its snout from side to side to kill or stun small fish. It can also use it in self defense.

SHARK SAVVY

Rays and Chimeras

• Chimeras live mainly in deep, cold areas of the sea.
• Unlike most sharks, which give birth to fully formed young, female chimeras lay egg cases, usually on the seabed. Many ray species also lay egg cases. The embryos develop within the egg cases and most hatch after about six to nine months.
• The guitarfish is the most similar ray to a shark.
• A few species of ray live in fresh water. The South American freshwater stingray lives in the Amazon River.
• The Javanese cownose ray congregates in schools of up to 1,000 rays.

SHAPE AND FORM

A shark's body shape provides clues to the way it lives. A shark with a sleek, torpedo-shaped body will spend much of its life swimming. A shark with a flattened body will spend more of its time resting on the sea floor. The various fins each have a special purpose. The main swimming power comes from the tail, or caudal fin. The side-to-side movement of the tail pushes the shark forward through the water. The dorsal fin and anal fins help prevent the shark from rolling over to the side. The pectoral and pelvic fins lift the front of the body and are used for turning. The rough texture of a shark's skin is caused by thousands of tiny teethlike scales, called dermal denticles.

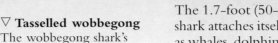

▽ **Tasselled wobbegong**
The wobbegong shark's body color and fleshy head tassels provide perfect camouflage for hiding on the seabed.

COOKIE CUTTER
The 1.7-foot (50-cm) long cookie cutter shark attaches itself to large animals such as whales, dolphins, and tuna. It attaches itself using its lips, which form a suction cup. Then it bites and swivels its body around to cut out an oval-shaped plug of tissue, just like a pastry cutter.

BOTTOM DWELLERS
Unlike most sharks, nurse sharks, dogfish, and other bottom-dwelling sharks do not need to swim continuously to breathe. Many have muscular gill slits, which help to pump water over the gills when the shark is resting. The spiracle, a special opening behind each eye, provides oxygen to the eye and brain.

◁ **Skin teeth**
Dermal denticles give the shark a flexible armor, which also improves the shark's streamlining.

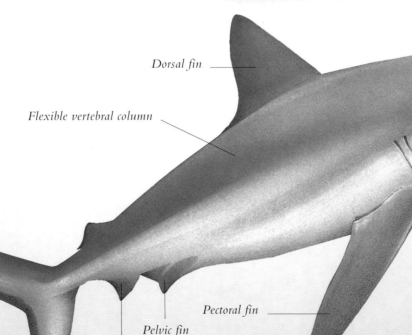

Spiracle   *Skull*

Dorsal fin

Flexible vertebral column

Gill arches

Gill slits

Caudal fin

▷ **Shark teeth**
A shark may use and discard thousands of teeth in its lifetime. When a tooth is lost, it is replaced after a few days from the row behind.

Pectoral fin

Pelvic fin

Anal fin

SKELETON, TEETH, AND MUSCLES
The parts of a shark's skeleton that have to cope with physical stress, such as the skull and vertebrae, are stiffened with calcium. Worn or broken front teeth are continuously replaced by new teeth growing in rows behind them. The muscles are attached to the shark's tough skin, which makes them work very efficiently.

PROTECTIVE EYELID

Most sharks have eyelids that do not close. Some sharks, especially members of the order carcharhiniformes (*see page 4*), have a movable lower eyelid called a nictating membrane. This tough eyelid moves up to cover the shark's eye when it is feeding, to protect it from damage.

▽ **Lantern shark**
At only 8 inches (20 cm) long, the lantern shark may be one of the smallest sharks, but it is able to glow in the dark!

LIGHTING UP

Some deepwater sharks, such as the lantern shark, have special light-producing cells, called photophores. They produce a weak light that matches the faint light from the surface, helping to camouflage the shark. This is called bioluminescence. The pattern produced by some lantern sharks differs from male to female, which helps them to find a mate.

see page 4

SHARK SAVVY

Tail Shapes

- The great white shark's symmetrical tail is good for bursts of speed.
- The nurse shark's tail is good for slow swimming.
- The longer top lobe of the tiger shark's tail gives extra maneuverability.

Great white shark

Nurse shark

Tiger shark

SPIRAL STOMACH

The inside of a shark's stomach is in a spiral shape, like a spiral staircase. The spiral shape takes up less space inside the body, slows the movement of food, and increases the surface area of the stomach through which nutrients can be absorbed by the body.

Brain

Heart

Liver

Spiral valve

LIVER AND GILLS

One of the largest organs is the shark's oily liver. This is essential in helping to keep the shark buoyant, because sharks do not have a gas-filled swim bladder, like bony fish. The gills extract vital oxygen from the water, which is pumped around the body by the heart.

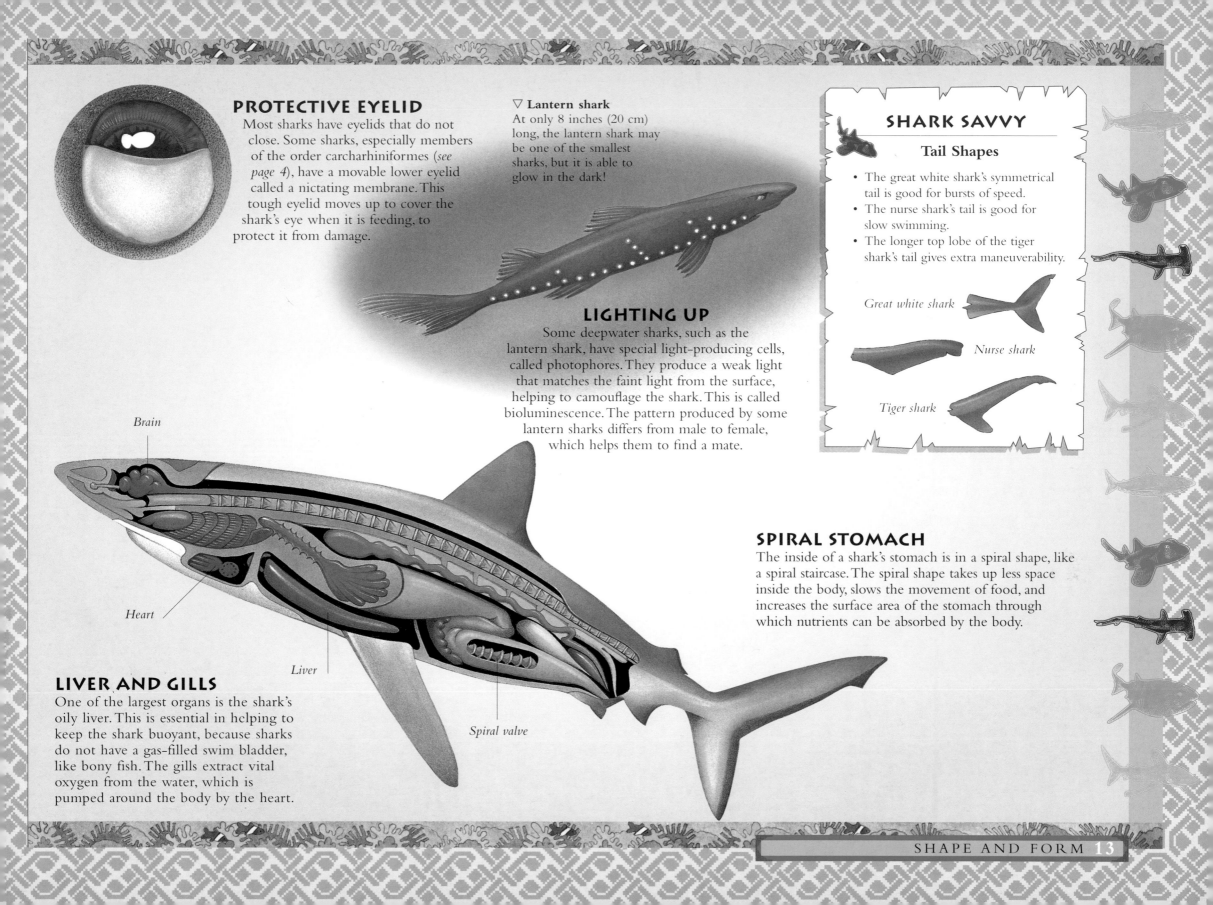

SHARK BEHAVIOR

Sharks are not easy subjects to study. They often range over a wide area and scientists can only spend a limited time in the water, so most of what we know about shark behavior is based on studies of only a few species. However, what we have learned has helped to dispel some of the myths surrounding sharks. We once thought of sharks as lone hunters cruising the oceans, little more than eating machines in search of something to munch on. Recent studies have revealed complex shark behavior involving interaction with other sharks, feeding, and mating. In many marine habitats, several species, or even groups of the same species of shark, exist side by side.

NONAGGRESSIVE BEHAVIOR

Normal posture

Normal posture

AGGRESSIVE BEHAVIOR

Raised head

Hunched back

THREAT DISPLAY

When a gray reef shark is upset by another shark, or a diver, it performs a threat display (*see left*). Instead of swimming normally, the shark hunches its back, raises its head, and points its pectoral fins downward. This makes the shark swim awkwardly and displays its aggression. The more the shark is upset, the more exaggerated the posture becomes. Few sharks give such clear signals that they may attack.

TAIL FISHING

The thresher shark uses its extraordinarily long tail to catch fish. The shark slaps the water surface with its tail to frighten fish into a tight group, making it easier to catch them. The shark may even use its tail to stun prey. Sometimes, two thresher sharks work together to herd fish together before both sharks lunge into the shoal (group of fish) to feast.

▽ **Common thresher shark**
The common thresher shark may have a tail up to 20 feet (6 meters) long.

◁ **Hammerhead schools**
Schools containing hundreds of scallop hammerheads gather around undersea mountains in the Gulf of California.

PECKING ORDER

A dead whale often attracts large numbers of sharks. The largest sharks feed first, while the smaller ones circle a little way off. When the large sharks have finished feeding, the smaller sharks move in to feed. This pecking order helps reduce the chances of a smaller shark being attacked by a larger one.

PEST CONTROL

On tropical reefs, special fish help remove irritating parasites from sharks and other large fish. These fish are collectively known as "cleaner fish" and are usually wrasse or butterfly fish. As the sharks cruise slowly around the area, the cleaner fish remove the parasites by eating them. Both the cleaner fish and the sharks benefit from this special relationship.

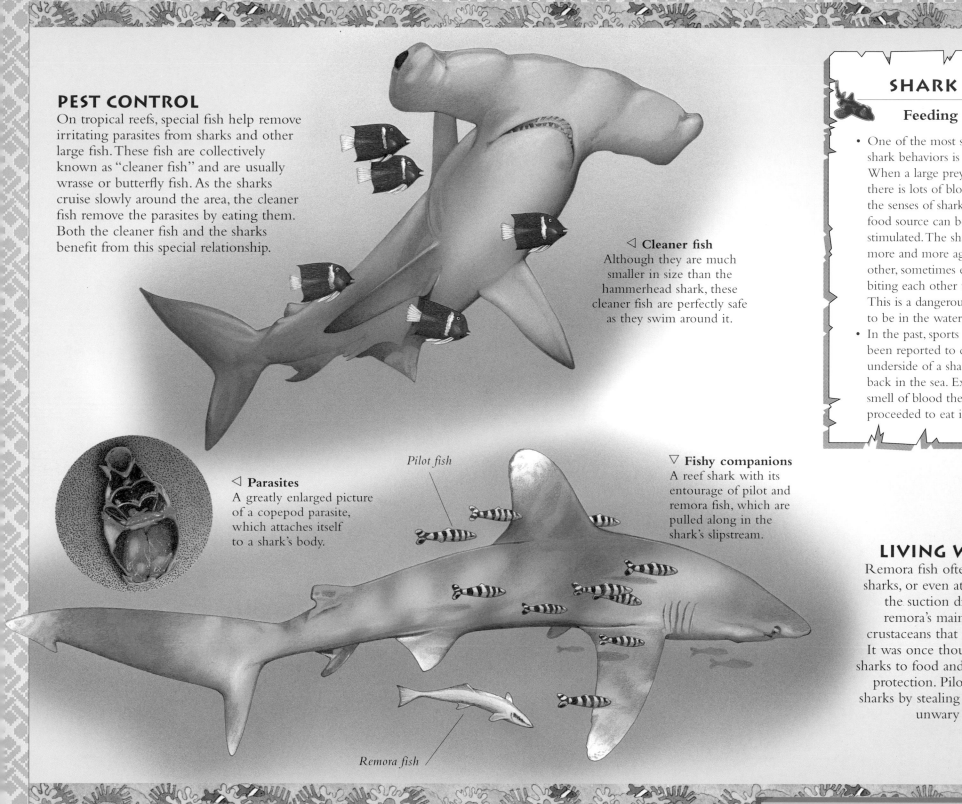

◁ **Cleaner fish**
Although they are much smaller in size than the hammerhead shark, these cleaner fish are perfectly safe as they swim around it.

◁ **Parasites**
A greatly enlarged picture of a copepod parasite, which attaches itself to a shark's body.

Pilot fish

▽ **Fishy companions**
A reef shark with its entourage of pilot and remora fish, which are pulled along in the shark's slipstream.

Remora fish

LIVING WITH SHARKS

Remora fish often swim close to large sharks, or even attach themselves using the suction disk on their head. The remora's main diet is small parasitic crustaceans that infest the shark's skin. It was once thought that pilot fish led sharks to food and in return were given protection. Pilot fish do benefit from sharks by stealing scraps of food, but an unwary straggler will become the shark's next meal!

SHARK SENSES

The world of the shark is three-dimensional, although often dark and murky. Sharks have amazing senses, including smell, vision, hearing, and electrical, which they use to explore this watery world. The senses are used to help find their way around, locate food, and avoid danger. When hunting, the senses are often used together first to find and then to catch prey, different senses coming into play as the shark gets nearer to its quarry. A better awareness of a shark's senses and how it uses them may help us to understand and avoid shark attacks on humans.

▷ **A shark's brain**
Different areas of the brain receive and process information from the various senses. Fast-swimming sharks have larger brains than bottom-living species, probably to interpret the extra information.

SMELL

Sharks have a sharp sense of smell. This helps bottom-living sharks to find prey hidden beneath the sand, or larger sharks stalking an injured animal. Sharks can detect the minute trail left by an injured fish equal to one drop of fish blood in more than a million drops of seawater.

◁ **Horn shark**
The nostrils of the horn shark have evolved into elaborate folds. These give the maximum surface area for detecting faint odors.

LATERAL LINE

Like most fish, sharks have a special sense organ called the lateral line system, which detects the water movements made by prey or predators. The lateral line is made up of a series of pores along the shark's body, tail, and head. The pores lead to sensory hair cells just beneath the skin. The slightest pressure created by the movement of prey or predators alerts the shark to its location depending on which part of the lateral line detects it.

▷ **Injured prey**
Sharks will often home in on the blood trail from an injured animal such as a fish. As the shark swims nearer, it will sense the stronger vibrations caused by the struggling fish.

Lens

△ Shark eye
The eyeball of a shark is oval shaped. The lens can be moved by muscles to focus an image on the retina.

Retina

NIGHT VISION

Sharks have highly sensitive eyes, which can see extremely well in the dim light of dusk, night, and dawn, when many species hunt. Behind the retina, the part where the image is formed, the eye has a reflective layer that reflects the light back to the light receptor cells, increasing the sensitivity of the eye.

HEARING

A shark's hearing is particularly sensitive to low-pitched sounds, like the movement of a fish or a swimmer. Sound waves traveling through the water enter the shark's body through two special pores and travel down to the inner ears. Three fluid-filled, semicircular canals provide a sense of balance.

Sensory pore

Inner ear underneath the sensory pores

TYPES OF EYES

Sharks' eyes vary between species. The fast-swimming blue shark and hammerhead have large eyes on the sides of their head. The bottom-living Port Jackson shark has relatively small eyes since it relies mainly on smell and its electrical sense on the seabed. The tiny cookie cutter shark has large eyes to help it to see in the dark ocean depths.

Hammerhead

Blue shark

Port Jackson

Cookie cutter

△ Specialization
The size, shape, and position of the eyes vary between shark species according to where they live in the sea and how they hunt.

ELECTRICAL SENSE

Sharks can detect the electrical signals created by underwater animals using sensory pores on their snout. The shark must be within 3.3 feet (1 meter) to sense the electrical field, but injured prey can be detected up to 10 feet (3 meters) away because electrical signals leak out from the wound.

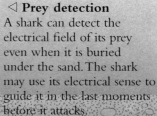

◁ Prey detection
A shark can detect the electrical field of its prey even when it is buried under the sand. The shark may use its electrical sense to guide it in the last moments before it attacks.

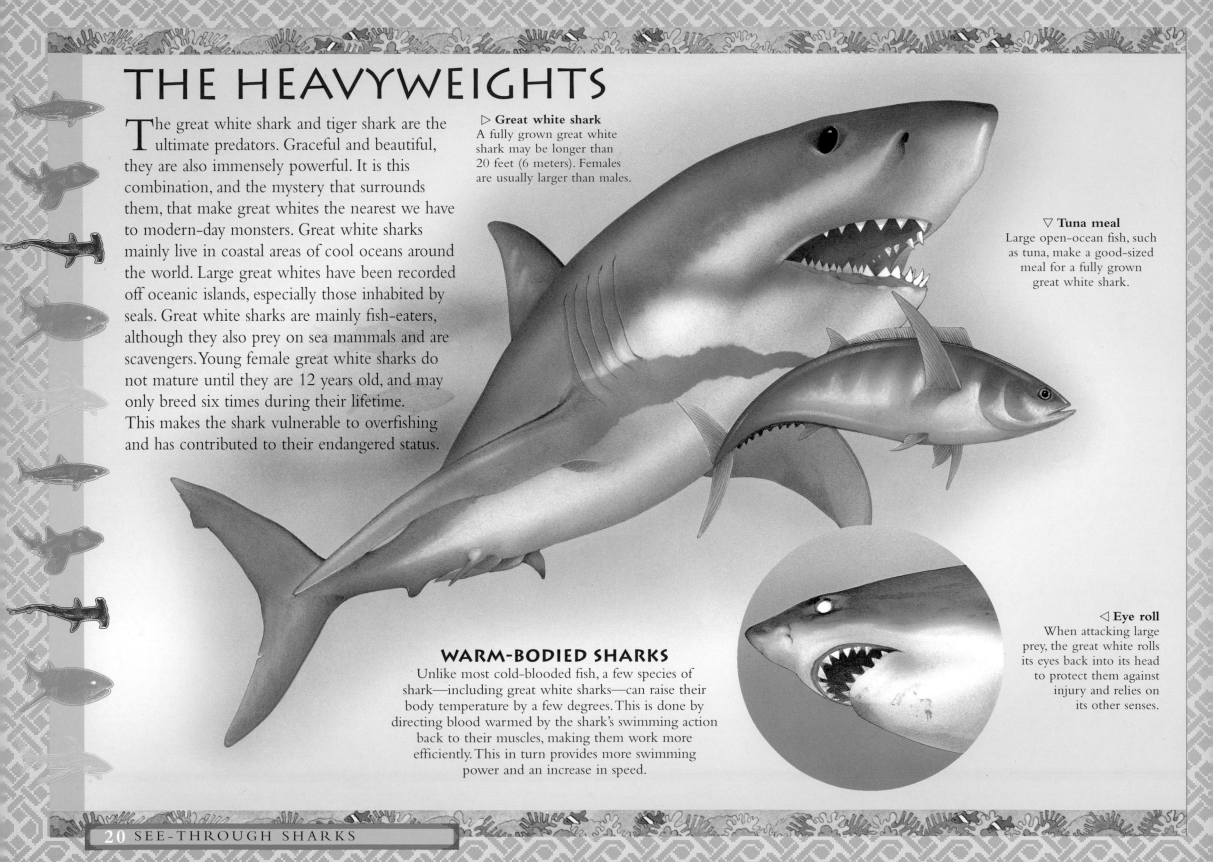

THE HEAVYWEIGHTS

The great white shark and tiger shark are the ultimate predators. Graceful and beautiful, they are also immensely powerful. It is this combination, and the mystery that surrounds them, that make great whites the nearest we have to modern-day monsters. Great white sharks mainly live in coastal areas of cool oceans around the world. Large great whites have been recorded off oceanic islands, especially those inhabited by seals. Great white sharks are mainly fish-eaters, although they also prey on sea mammals and are scavengers. Young female great white sharks do not mature until they are 12 years old, and may only breed six times during their lifetime. This makes the shark vulnerable to overfishing and has contributed to their endangered status.

▷ **Great white shark**
A fully grown great white shark may be longer than 20 feet (6 meters). Females are usually larger than males.

▽ **Tuna meal**
Large open-ocean fish, such as tuna, make a good-sized meal for a fully grown great white shark.

◁ **Eye roll**
When attacking large prey, the great white rolls its eyes back into its head to protect them against injury and relies on its other senses.

WARM-BODIED SHARKS

Unlike most cold-blooded fish, a few species of shark—including great white sharks—can raise their body temperature by a few degrees. This is done by directing blood warmed by the shark's swimming action back to their muscles, making them work more efficiently. This in turn provides more swimming power and an increase in speed.

▽ **Cage diving**
The safest way to observe great white sharks in their own element is from inside a steel cage.

▷ **Shark gods**
Shark legends mainly occur in the Pacific Island cultures. This statue of a shark god shows its human form.

GODS AND DEMONS

In the past, many cultures that relied on the ocean for a living shared it with sharks. To some, sharks were a blessing; to others, a menace. In Hawaii, sharks were seen as protectors, but in some South American cultures they were considered demons. Other cultures hunted them for food, and to make tools and weapons.

SHARK ATTACKS

Only six shark species pose any real threat to humans: the great white, tiger, bull, oceanic whitetip, mako, and blue. Of these, the great white is to blame for many of the shark attacks that occur in cool seas. Our fear of great white sharks is magnified by our sense of vulnerability in the ocean. And as leisure activities such as diving, surfing, and windsurfing increase, more people are brought into contact with sharks.

◁ **Tiger shark**
The tiger shark grows to at least 18 feet (5.5 meters) long. It is named after its striped body markings.

ANYTHING GOES

Tiger sharks have one of the widest-ranging diets, including sea turtles, dolphins, and poisonous prey such as stingrays, sea snakes, and jellyfish. The tiger shark is second only to the great white in the number of reported attacks on humans. Objects found inside a dead shark's stomach include car license plates, bottles of wine, and rubber tires.

EASY PREY

Like all other living things, sharks need energy to stay alive. The energy comes from their food, and sharks are very efficient at finding and catching prey. Sharks have adapted to life in many parts of the ocean and have evolved feeding techniques to catch the animals that live there. Between all the species, sharks feed on a very diverse range of food. Some bottom-living sharks feed on fish, crustaceans, and mollusks that live on the seabed. A handful of species filter seawater for tiny organisms. Some are hunters of fish and squid, while others tackle larger prey such as seals and dolphins. Sharks often feed on weak and sick animals, which helps to maintain a healthy ocean.

ON THE PROWL

A cruising great white shark detects the presence of prey nearby. It slowly circles, gathering more information about its target from its various senses. The shark's movements disturb a shoal of small fish, which it ignores, although the fish attract the attention of seabirds eager for an easy meal. The shark's fin breaks the surface and then disappears.

MOVABLE JAWS

Great white sharks are able to eat prey much bigger than their mouth, such as a tuna or the carcass of a dead whale. As the shark opens its mouth to bite, the top jaw moves forward, the snout is lifted up, and the lower jaw swings down.

△ **Blue shark**
The graceful blue shark cruises slowly, feeding on fish and squid that migrate to the ocean's surface at night.

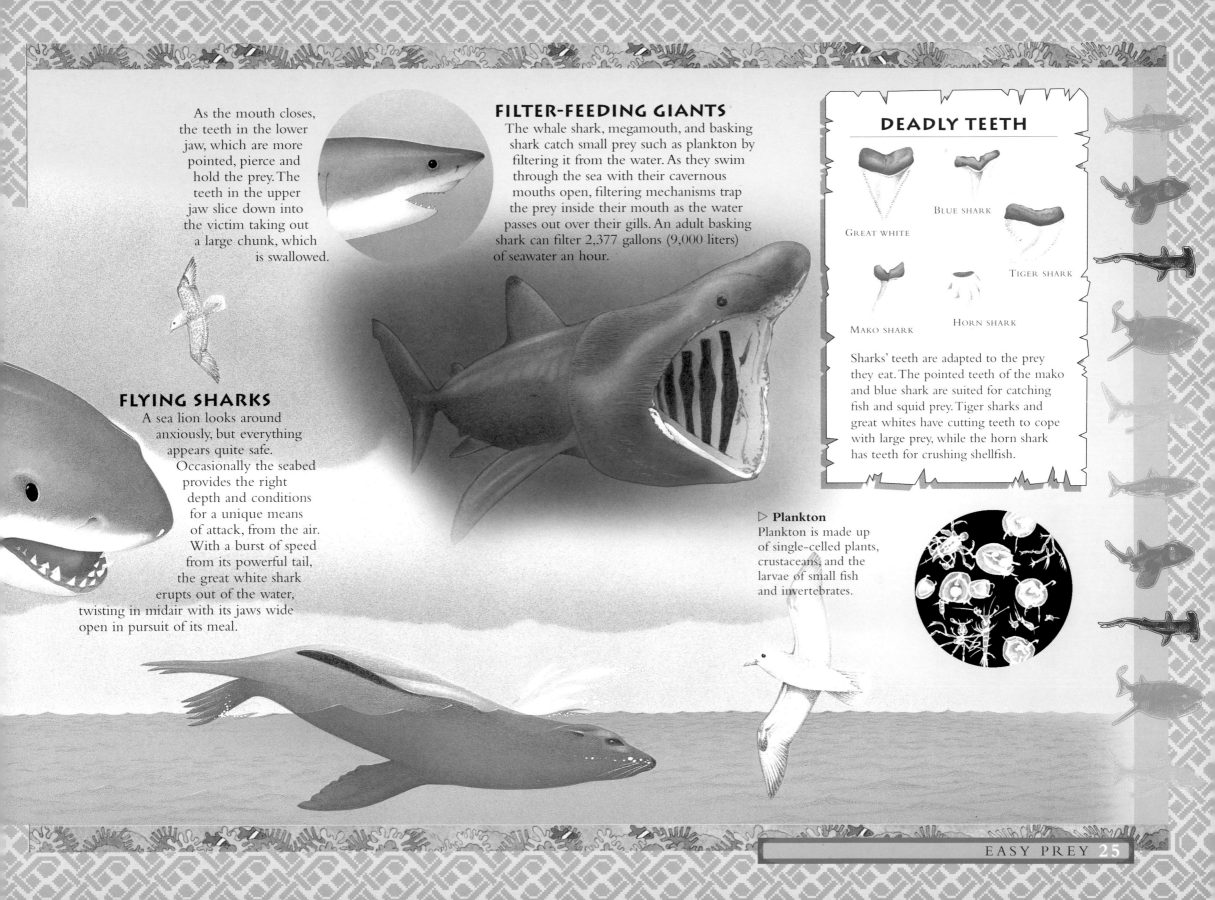

As the mouth closes, the teeth in the lower jaw, which are more pointed, pierce and hold the prey. The teeth in the upper jaw slice down into the victim taking out a large chunk, which is swallowed.

FILTER-FEEDING GIANTS

The whale shark, megamouth, and basking shark catch small prey such as plankton by filtering it from the water. As they swim through the sea with their cavernous mouths open, filtering mechanisms trap the prey inside their mouth as the water passes out over their gills. An adult basking shark can filter 2,377 gallons (9,000 liters) of seawater an hour.

DEADLY TEETH

GREAT WHITE

BLUE SHARK

TIGER SHARK

MAKO SHARK

HORN SHARK

Sharks' teeth are adapted to the prey they eat. The pointed teeth of the mako and blue shark are suited for catching fish and squid prey. Tiger sharks and great whites have cutting teeth to cope with large prey, while the horn shark has teeth for crushing shellfish.

FLYING SHARKS

A sea lion looks around anxiously, but everything appears quite safe. Occasionally the seabed provides the right depth and conditions for a unique means of attack, from the air. With a burst of speed from its powerful tail, the great white shark erupts out of the water, twisting in midair with its jaws wide open in pursuit of its meal.

▷ **Plankton**
Plankton is made up of single-celled plants, crustaceans, and the larvae of small fish and invertebrates.

REPRODUCTION

Most fish produce thousands or even millions of tiny eggs, many of which will be eaten by other fish before they have a chance to hatch. Even if they survive to hatch, many young fish are eaten before they reach full size. Sharks have developed a different technique. The female either gives birth to fully developed baby sharks, called pups, or she lays the eggs in tough cases attached to underwater objects. When they are born or hatch from their egg cases, the pups are much bigger than other baby fish and are better equipped to survive the many dangers a young shark must face.

COURTSHIP

The courtship of reef sharks can be quite an aggressive affair, with the male biting the female's body and fins. The male has two claspers to help him mate, which have developed from the pelvic fins.

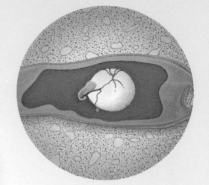

△ **Egg case**
The yolk inside a swell shark's egg case provides all the food the baby shark needs to grow.

EGG LAYERS

Sharks that lay eggs are called oviparous. The eggs are encased in a leathery protective shell, known as an egg case. Only one baby shark develops inside each egg case. Dogfish attach their eggs to seaweed and similar objects by twisting themselves around them. Zebra shark egg cases have sticky filaments, which glue the egg to the seabed.

LIVE YOUNG

Most sharks are viviparous, which means they give birth to live young. The eggs of these sharks remain inside the female shark's body. Here they are nourished by the egg yolk, which is attached to the baby shark by a yolk stalk. The young are born when all the egg yolk has been absorbed. The young of a few shark species receive nutrients directly from the mother when the yolk is used up.

▷ **Dogfish development**
A male dogfish curls its body around a female during courtship. The female lays her eggs two at a time.

△ Hatching
The baby swell shark continues to grow until all the yolk has been used up. It leaves the egg case through a slit at the end.

△ Cannibalism
A few shark species produce thousands of small eggs, which become food for the first few that hatch while still inside the female.

A HEAD START

Baby sharks develop for many months inside the egg case, depending on the species and the temperature of the surrounding water. When they hatch, the pups are miniature replicas of the adults and can feed almost immediately. The upper part of their body is colored to help them blend in with their surroundings.

BIG BROODS

The broods of some live-bearing sharks are relatively big. The blue shark produces litters of more than 100 pups, while the enormous whale shark gives birth to as many as 300. Some shark species appear to give birth in shallow nursery areas, where they are less likely to be eaten by larger sharks.

◁ Dogfish development
The young dogfish develop within the egg cases, secured safely to seaweed. After about nine months the egg cases hatch and the baby dogfish swim away.

STUDYING SHARKS

There are many things that we do not know about sharks, and scientists around the world are trying to find out more. One thing they have discovered is that sharks play an important role in food chains. For example, without the great white shark to prey on them, sea lions would multiply. The sea lions would eat more fish, which would deprive other sea animals and fishermen of their catch. Many sharks are threatened either by commercial fishing, sports fishing, or by persecution. Apart from the meat, sharks are hunted for their skin, liver oil, or their fins to make shark fin soup. It has been estimated that for every person killed by a shark, roughly 10 million sharks are killed by humans.

▽ **Shark jaws**
Large sharks are often killed for their jaws, which are used as trophies or sold for their novelty value.

TEETH TRADE

Shark teeth have been used for decoration and jewelry for thousands of years. Today, shark jaws and teeth are sold as curios and ornaments around the world. As the fascination for sharks increases, so has the demand for these items, which puts added pressure on shark populations that are already threatened.

▽ **Swimming speed**
A special propeller attached to a recording device measures how fast a shark moves through the water.

MOVING AROUND

By attaching tags to sharks, scientists have discovered that many large sharks travel long distances in search of food or to mate. The record holder for the longest distance traveled was a blue shark, which swam 3,714 miles (5,980 km) from Brazil to New York. The more we learn about how sharks behave, the better chance we will have of preventing shark attacks.

△ **Shark encounters**
By following strict rules, diving with sharks is rewarding but also safe for the divers and the sharks.

SWIMMING WITH SHARKS

A planned encounter with sharks is a thrilling experience. There are an increasing number of dive operators worldwide offering the chance to swim with sharks. These range from snorkeling with an awesome whale shark to cage diving with a great white. People can also record what they see on dives, which can add to our knowledge of sharks.

SPORTS FISHING

Large, powerful sharks are often caught by game fishermen for the challenge of fighting them on a rod and line by physical force alone. Since only the biggest shark catches are recorded, the actual number of sharks caught by recreational fishermen is unknown.

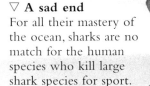

▽ **A sad end**
For all their mastery of the ocean, sharks are no match for the human species who kill large shark species for sport.

COMMERCIAL FISHING

As populations of traditional commercial fish have declined, the number of sharks and rays that are caught for human consumption has increased. It has been estimated that almost 350,000 tons of sharks are caught each year. The most wasteful type of fishing is for shark fins, to make shark fin soup. After the fin is removed, the rest of the shark is thrown back in the sea.

▷ **Shark nets**
A hammerhead shark is entangled in a net designed to protect bathing beaches in Australia and Africa.

CHANGING ATTITUDES

Public aquariums can help change people's attitudes toward sharks. As people see the sharks swimming safely behind glass, it is easier for them to appreciate their grace and beauty. This will hopefully lead to the protection of more sharks.

△ **Aquariums**
In a public aquarium people can come face to face with a shark without the fear that they may become its next meal.

SHARK SAVVY

Overfishing

- Recent research suggests that the current levels of shark fishing for food and sport is not sustainable.
- Sustainable fishing means that the number of new sharks being born replaces the number of sharks killed through fishing.
- If shark fishing is not sustainable, the number of sharks will drop and they may become endangered. They may even become extinct.
- Many shark species produce only a few young in their lifetime. Female sharks are often caught before they have the opportunity to mate and produce young.

GLOSSARY AND INDEX

anal fins Situated on the underside, toward the back, these fins help to keep the shark from rolling sideways, with the help of the dorsal fin.

backbone The row of bones that runs down the middle of the back. Also called the spine.

barbel The long, thin, fleshy growth that hangs from the mouth of some bottom-living fish—used for sensing.

bioluminescence The production of light (but not heat) by living things, such as deepwater creatures.

bony fish A fish that has a skeleton made from bone.

buoyant Able to float in water, not sink.

camouflage To be colored or shaped in such a way as to match the surrounding area, for example, the seabed.

cartilage A light, bendy material that a shark's skeleton is made of. Our ear lobes are also made of cartilage.

cartilaginous Something that is made of cartilage.

caudal fin Another name for the tail.

claspers Paired organs of the male shark used to aid reproduction.

cloaca Body cavity opening for reproductive organs and passing body waste.

dermal denticles Tiny toothlike structures that cover a shark's body and provide protection.

dorsal fin Large fin on the back of a fish that provides stability. Some fish, including sharks, may have two dorsal fins.

egg case Leathery protection that surrounds the egg of a shark or ray.

embryo An animal in the early stages of development before it is born.

evolve To change gradually over time (e.g. thousands of years) and develop features that increase survival.

extinct An animal (or plant) that once lived but has now died out.

feeding frenzy This occurs when lots of sharks are attracted by blood and food—this overloads their senses and causes them to get excited.

gills The branched breathing organs of a fish that extract oxygen from water.

gill slits Openings in the side of the head of a shark that allow water to flow back into the sea.

habitat The natural home of an animal or plant.

invertebrate An animal without a backbone, such as a snail or a crab.

lateral line A line of pores on the side of a fish's body that is sensitive to vibrations and changes in water pressure.

light receptor cells Special cells that are sensitive to light.

mammal A warm-blooded animal with a backbone, such as a horse or a seal.

megalodon An extinct species of shark similar to, but larger than, a great white shark.

nictating membrane A special third eyelid that protects the eyes of some types of shark when they are feeding.

order A way of classifying a group of animals (or plants) that is further subdivided into families and then species.

overfishing When a much larger number of fish are caught than are being born to replace them.

parasites An animal (or plant) that receives its nourishment by living within or on another living thing.

pectoral fins Positioned on the side of the body, just behind the head, these fins help to provide lift.

pelvic fin These fins are on the underside of a fish and aid movement.

predatory Hunting and feeding on another animal.

prehistoric A time before history was recorded.

prey Animals that are hunted and killed by other animals.

pups The newly born/hatched young of some animals. A newborn shark, seal, or dog is called a pup.

retina The light-sensitive inner layer at the back of the eyeball.

scavengers An animal that feeds on other dead animals or organic matter.

schools A term for a group of fish swimming together.

sensory pores Tiny openings that lead to sense cells.

slipstream The stream of water (or air) forced backward by, for example, a shark as it swims forward.

spiracle A small opening on the head of some sharks and rays.

streamlined Having a shape (like a shark's) that moves easily through the water.

swim bladder An air-filled sac that keeps a fish buoyant.

temperate Having a climate between tropical and polar.

threat display A display used to threaten others.

vertebrae Small bones that make up a vertebrate's backbone.

vertebrate An animal with a backbone.